PLAYER NAME:

WHO GOD SAYS
I AM

I am a child of God [Romans 8:14]

I have a calling and a purpose [Jeremiah 29:11]

I am the light of the world [Matthew 5:14]

I am victorious through Jesus [1 Corinthians 15:57]

I was chosen [Ephesians 1:4]

I am righteous and holy [Ephesians 2:24]

I can do all things [Philippians 4:13]

I am anointed by God [1 John 2:27]

I am loved [1 John 4:10]

I am a friend of God [John 15:15]

I have been given the mind of Christ [1 Corinthians 1:4]

Christ is in me [Colossians 1:27]

I am called [1 Corinthians 7:17]

I am free [Galatians 5:1]

I have God's peace [Philippians 4:19]

I am forgiven [1 John 1:9]

Use these affirmations to fill the "God Says..." section each day.

M T W TH F S SU

Date:

Start

God says ...

(▷) Today I am grateful for:

....

....

....

....

Today I feel:

....

....

....

TO DO

Today I will strive to be:

(▷) Top goal tomorrow:

....

....

....

....

M T W TH F S SU   Date:

Start

God says ...

▷ Today I am grateful for:

....

....

....

....

Today I feel:

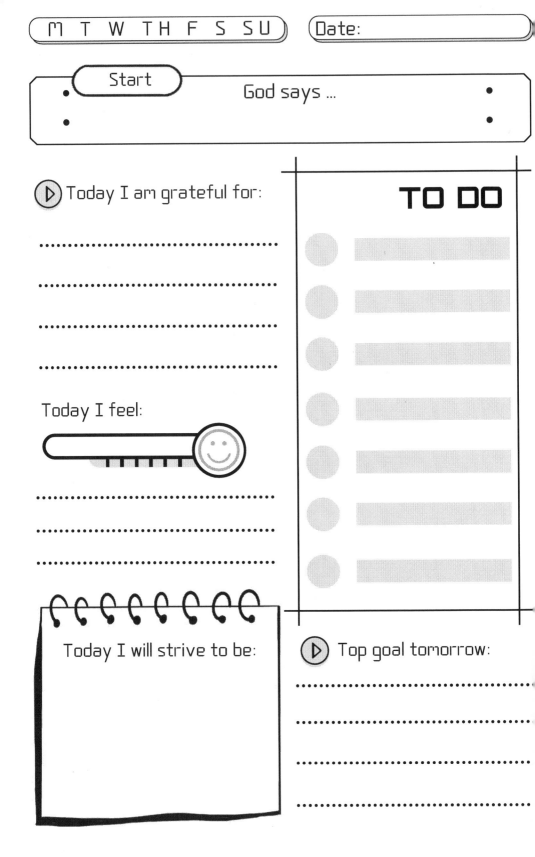

....

....

....

TO DO

Today I will strive to be:

▷ Top goal tomorrow:

....

....

....

....

M T W TH F S SU   Date:

Start   God says ...

▷ Today I am grateful for:

....

....

....

....

Today I feel:

....

....

....

Today I will strive to be:

TO DO

▷ Top goal tomorrow:

....

....

....

....

M T W TH F S SU   Date:

Start   God says ...
•   •
•   •

▷ Today I am grateful for: **TO DO**

....
....
....
....

Today I feel:

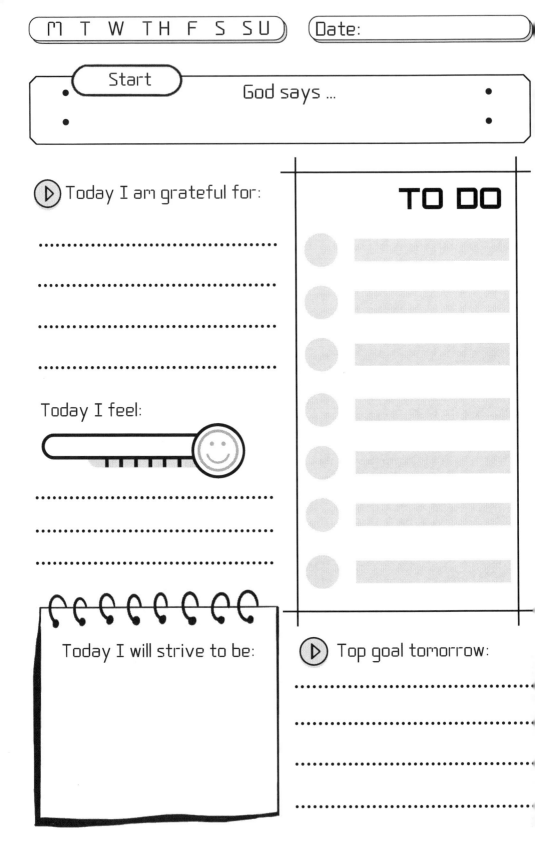

....
....
....

Today I will strive to be: ▷ Top goal tomorrow:

....
....
....
....

M T W TH F S SU   Date:

Start

God says ...

(▷) Today I am grateful for:

....

....

....

....

Today I feel:

....

....

....

TO DO

Today I will strive to be:

(▷) Top goal tomorrow:

....

....

....

....

M T W TH F S SU   Date:

Start

God says ...

▷ Today I am grateful for:

....

....

....

....

Today I feel:

....

....

....

TO DO

Today I will strive to be:

▷ Top goal tomorrow:

....

....

....

....

M   T   W   TH   F   S   SU   Date:

Start
• God says ...
•   •
                                                          •

(▷) Today I am grateful for:

....

....

....

....

Today I feel:

:)

....

....

....

Today I will strive to be:

TO DO

(▷) Top goal tomorrow:

....

....

....

....

M T W TH F S SU   Date:

Start   God says ...
•   •
•   •

▷ Today I am grateful for: **TO DO**

....

....

....

....

Today I feel:

🙂

....

....

....

Today I will strive to be: ▷ Top goal tomorrow:

....

....

....

....

M T W TH F S SU   Date:

Start
God says ...
•   •
•   •

▷ Today I am grateful for:

....

....

....

....

Today I feel:

:)

....

....

....

TO DO

Today I will strive to be:

▷ Top goal tomorrow:

....

....

....

....

M T W TH F S SU   Date:

Start

God says ...

▷ Today I am grateful for:

....

....

....

....

Today I feel:

....

....

....

TO DO

Today I will strive to be:

▷ Top goal tomorrow:

....

....

....

....

M T W TH F S SU   Date:

God says ...

-
-
-
-

Today I am grateful for:

....

....

....

....

Today I feel:

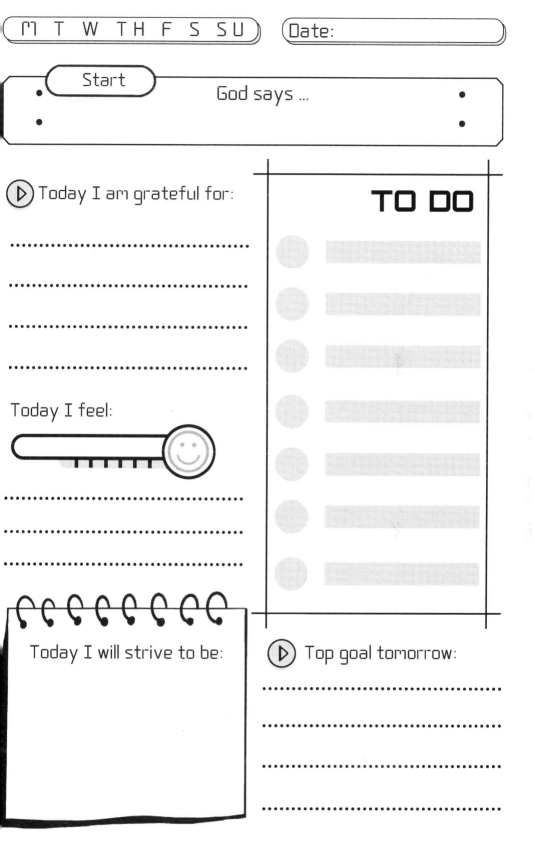

....

....

....

TO DO

Today I will strive to be:

Top goal tomorrow:

....

....

....

....

M T W TH F S SU   Date:

Start

God says ...

▷ Today I am grateful for:

....

....

....

....

Today I feel:

....

....

....

TO DO

Today I will strive to be:

▷ Top goal tomorrow:

....

....

....

....

M T W TH F S SU   Date:

Start
God says ...
•
•   •
                                               •

(▷) Today I am grateful for:

....

....

....

....

Today I feel:

....

....

....

Today I will strive to be:

TO DO

(▷) Top goal tomorrow:

....

....

....

....

M T W TH F S SU

Date:

Start

God says ...

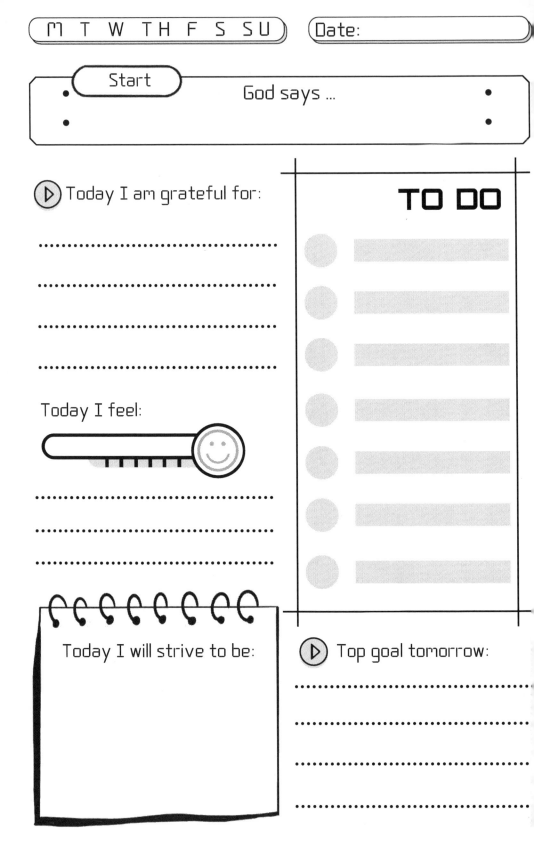 Today I am grateful for:

....

....

....

....

Today I feel:

....

....

....

TO DO

Today I will strive to be:

Top goal tomorrow:

....

....

....

....

M T W TH F S SU   Date:

Start

God says ...

▷ Today I am grateful for:

....

....

....

....

Today I feel:

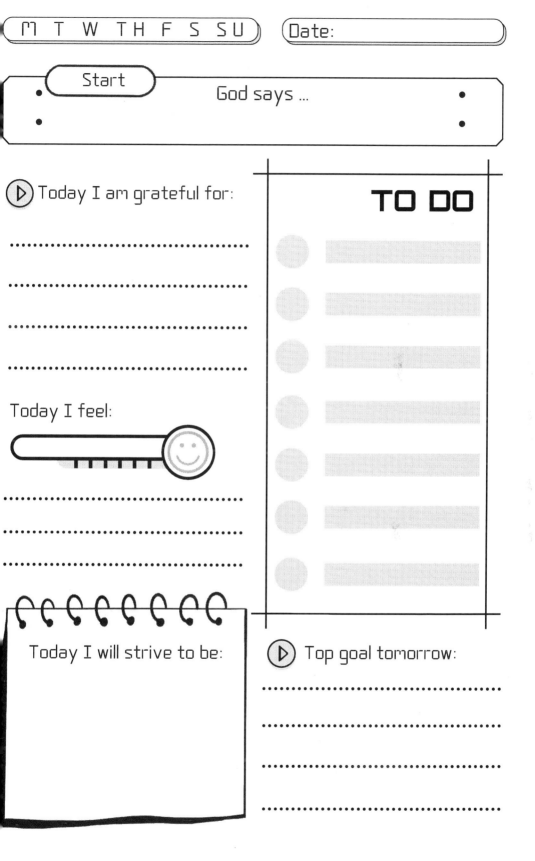

....

....

....

TO DO

Today I will strive to be:

▷ Top goal tomorrow:

....

....

....

....

M T W TH F S SU   Date:

Start   God says ...

▷ Today I am grateful for:

....

....

....

....

Today I feel:

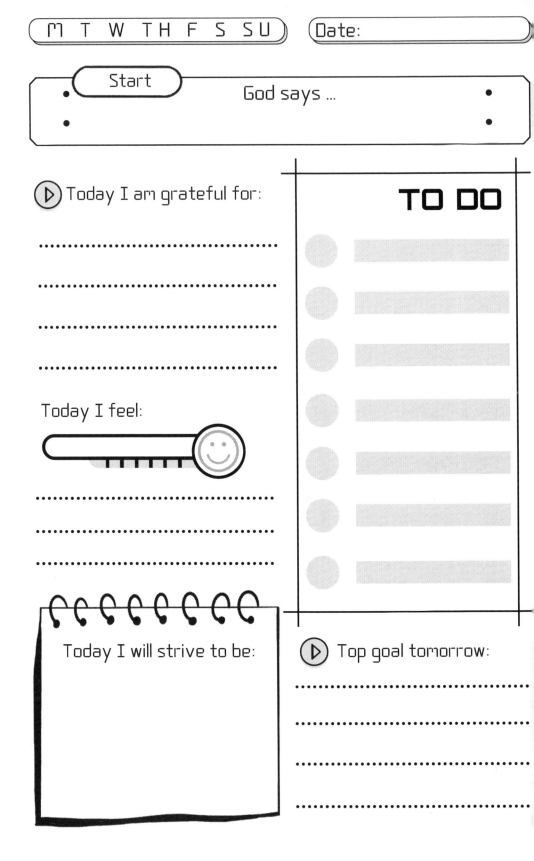

....

....

....

TO DO

Today I will strive to be:

▷ Top goal tomorrow:

....

....

....

....

M T W TH F S SU   Date:

Start   God says ...
•   •
•   •

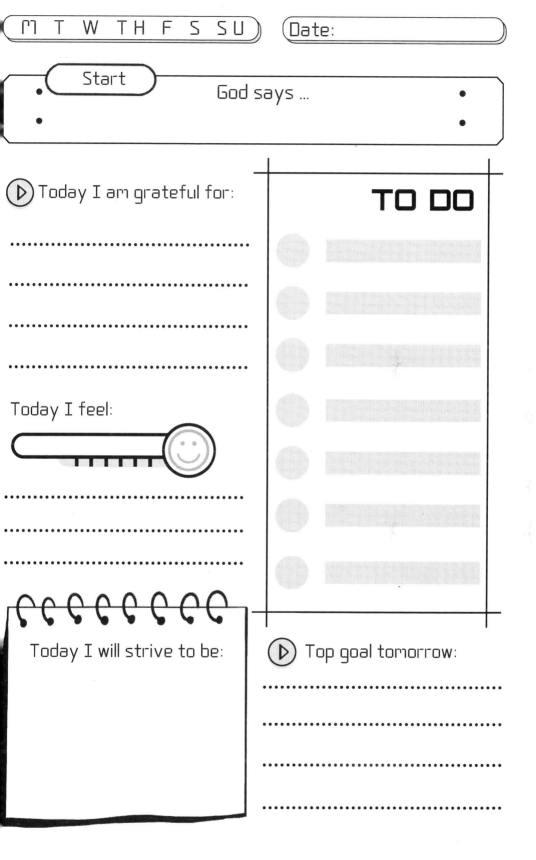

▷ Today I am grateful for: TO DO

....

....

....

....

Today I feel:

....

....

....

Today I will strive to be: ▷ Top goal tomorrow:

....

....

....

....

M T W TH F S SU   Date:

Start

God says ...

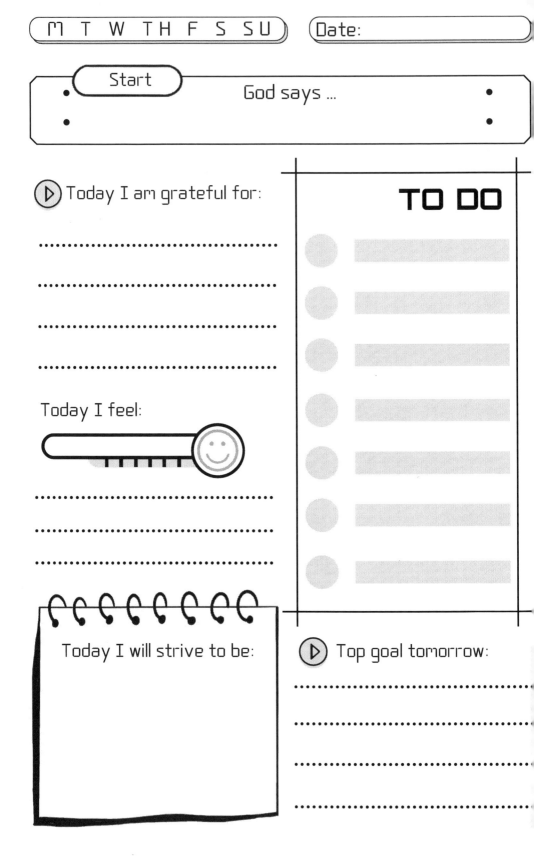

▷ Today I am grateful for:

....

....

....

....

Today I feel:

....

....

....

TO DO

Today I will strive to be:

▷ Top goal tomorrow:

....

....

....

....

M T W TH F S SU   Date:

Start   God says ...

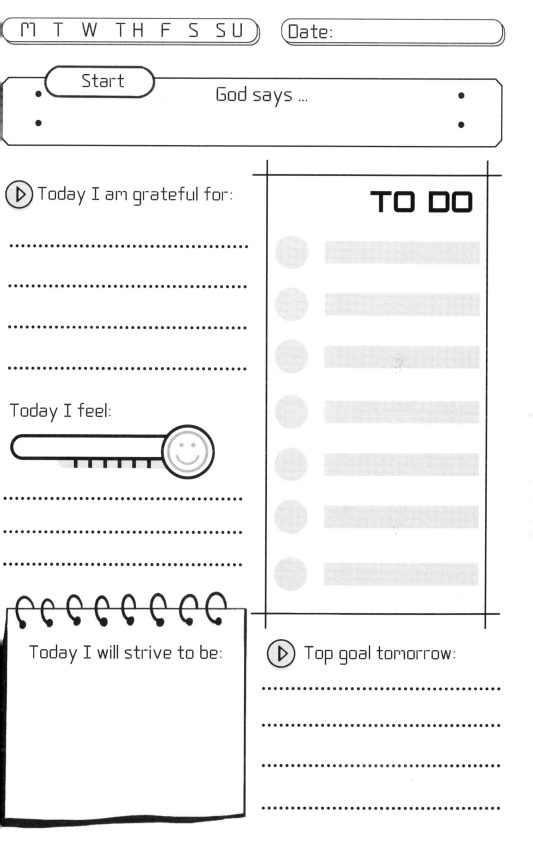

▷ Today I am grateful for:

....

....

....

....

Today I feel:

....

....

....

TO DO

Today I will strive to be:

▷ Top goal tomorrow:

....

....

....

....

M T W TH F S SU   Date:

Start

God says ...

▷ Today I am grateful for:

TO DO

....

....

....

....

Today I feel:

....

....

....

Today I will strive to be:

▷ Top goal tomorrow:

....

....

....

....

M T W TH F S SU | Date:

Start

God says ...

-
-
-
-

▷ Today I am grateful for:

....
....
....
....

Today I feel:

....
....
....

Today I will strive to be:

TO DO

▷ Top goal tomorrow:

....
....
....
....

M T W TH F S SU   Date:

Start   God says ...
•   •
•
•   •

▶ Today I am grateful for: **TO DO**

....   ○ ▢
....   ○ ▢
....   ○ ▢
....   ○ ▢

Today I feel: ○ ▢
                                               ○ ▢
....   ○ ▢
....
....

Today I will strive to be: ▶ Top goal tomorrow:

                                     ....
                                     ....
                                     ....
                                     ....

M T W TH F S SU   Date:

Start   God says ...
•   •
•   •

(▷) Today I am grateful for:

....

....

....

....

Today I feel:

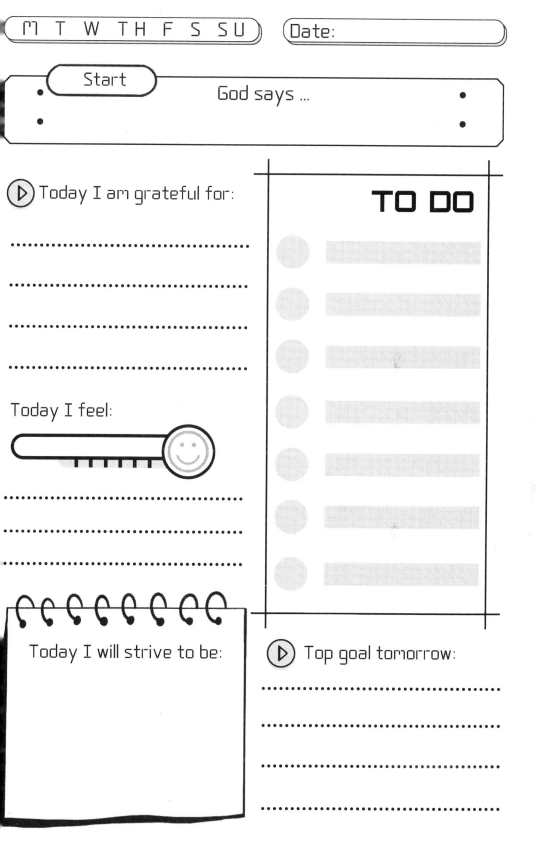

....

....

....

TO DO

Today I will strive to be: (▷) Top goal tomorrow:

....

....

....

....

Start

God says ...

▷ Today I am grateful for:

....

....

....

....

Today I feel:

....

....

....

TO DO

Today I will strive to be:

▷ Top goal tomorrow:

....

....

....

....

M T W TH F S SU   Date:

Start   God says ...
•   •
•   •

▷ Today I am grateful for:

....

....

....

....

Today I feel:

....

....

....

TO DO

○ ▭
○ ▭
○ ▭
○ ▭
○ ▭
○ ▭
○ ▭

Today I will strive to be:

▷ Top goal tomorrow:

....

....

....

....

M T W TH F S SU

Date:

Start

God says ...

▷ Today I am grateful for:

....

....

....

....

Today I feel:

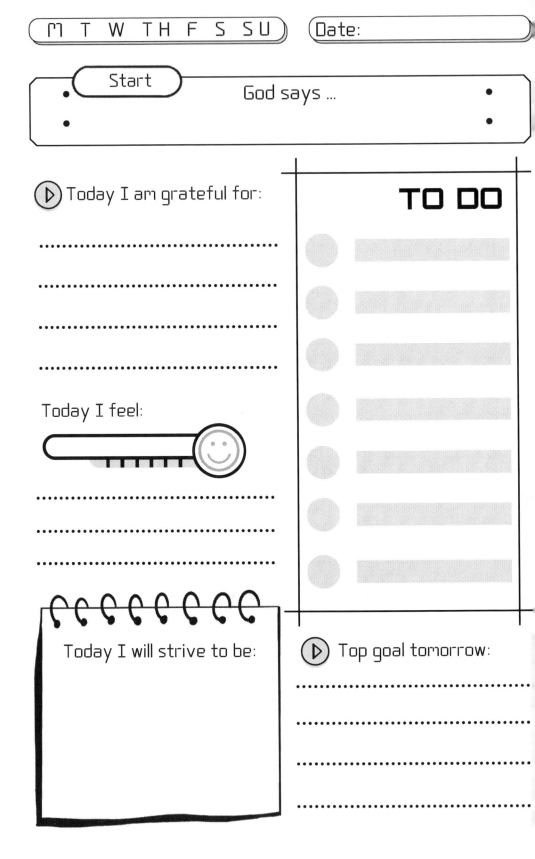

....

....

....

Today I will strive to be:

TO DO

▷ Top goal tomorrow:

....

....

....

....

M T W TH F S SU | Date:

God says ...

-
-

▷ Today I am grateful for:

....

....

....

....

Today I feel:

....

....

....

TO DO

Today I will strive to be:

▷ Top goal tomorrow:

....

....

....

....

M T W TH F S SU Date:

Start

God says ...

▷ Today I am grateful for:

....

....

....

....

Today I feel:

☺

....

....

....

TO DO

Today I will strive to be:

▷ Top goal tomorrow:

....

....

....

....

M T W TH F S SU   Date:

Start   God says ...
•
•   •
                                               •

(▷) Today I am grateful for: TO DO

....   ◯ ▭▭▭▭▭▭▭▭

....   ◯ ▭▭▭▭▭▭▭▭

....   ◯ ▭▭▭▭▭▭▭▭

....   ◯ ▭▭▭▭▭▭▭▭

Today I feel: ◯ ▭▭▭▭▭▭▭▭

                                          ◯ ▭▭▭▭▭▭▭▭

....   ◯ ▭▭▭▭▭▭▭▭
....
....

Today I will strive to be: (▷) Top goal tomorrow:

                                ....

                                ....

                                ....

                                ....

M T W TH F S SU   Date:

Start   God says ...
-
-
-   •
                                            •
                                            •

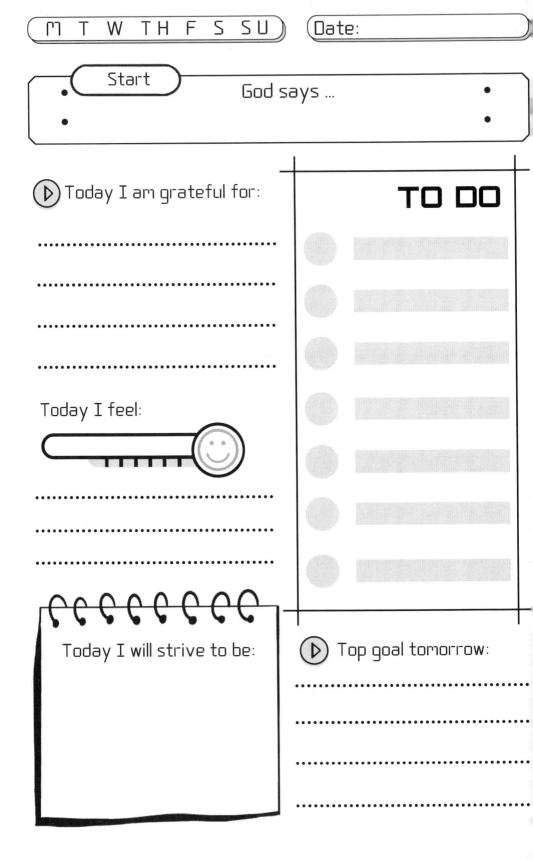

▷ Today I am grateful for:

....
....
....
....

Today I feel:

....
....
....

TO DO

Today I will strive to be:

▷ Top goal tomorrow:

....
....
....
....

M T W TH F S SU   Date:

Start   God says ...
•   •
•   •

▷ Today I am grateful for: TO DO

....

....

....

....

Today I feel:

😊

....

....

....

Today I will strive to be: ▷ Top goal tomorrow:

....

....

....

....

M T W TH F S SU | Date:

Start | God says ...

▷ Today I am grateful for:

....

....

....

....

Today I feel:

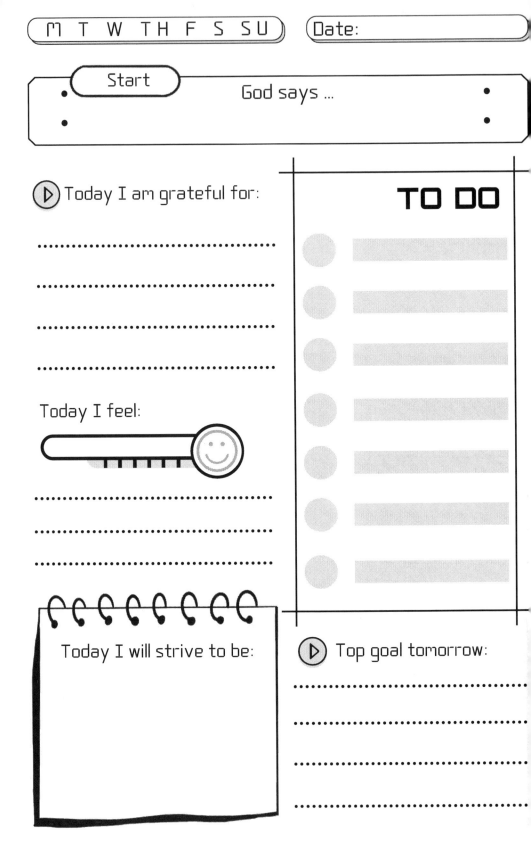

....

....

....

TO DO

Today I will strive to be:

▷ Top goal tomorrow:

....

....

....

....

M T W TH F S SU   Date:

Start

God says ...

▷ Today I am grateful for:

....

....

....

....

Today I feel:

....

....

....

TO DO

Today I will strive to be:

▷ Top goal tomorrow:

....

....

....

....

M T W TH F S SU

Date:

Start

God says ...

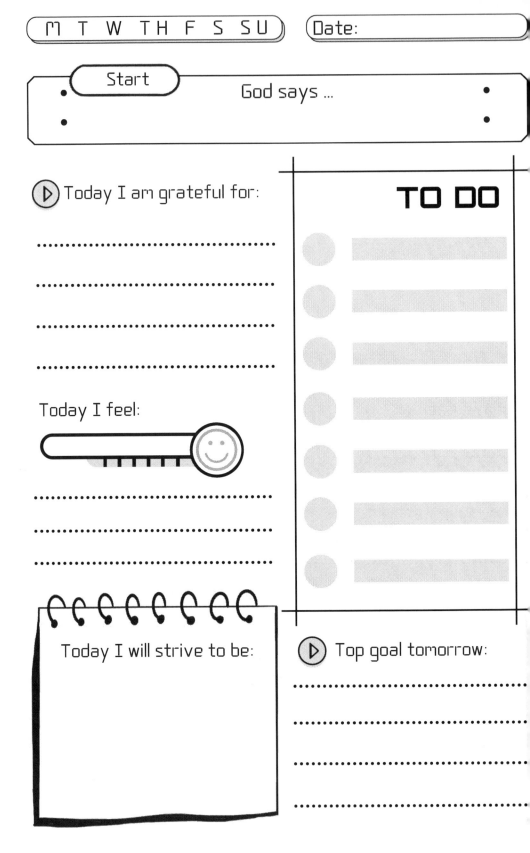

▷ Today I am grateful for:

....

....

....

....

Today I feel:

....

....

....

TO DO

Today I will strive to be:

▷ Top goal tomorrow:

....

....

....

....

M T W TH F S SU   Date:

Start

God says ...

▷ Today I am grateful for:

....

....

....

....

Today I feel:

....

....

....

TO DO

Today I will strive to be:

▷ Top goal tomorrow:

....

....

....

....

M T W TH F S SU   Date:

Start   God says ...
•   •
•   •

▷ Today I am grateful for: **TO DO**

....   ⬤ ▬▬▬▬▬▬▬▬▬

....   ⬤ ▬▬▬▬▬▬▬▬▬

....   ⬤ ▬▬▬▬▬▬▬▬▬

....   ⬤ ▬▬▬▬▬▬▬▬▬

Today I feel: ⬤ ▬▬▬▬▬▬▬▬▬

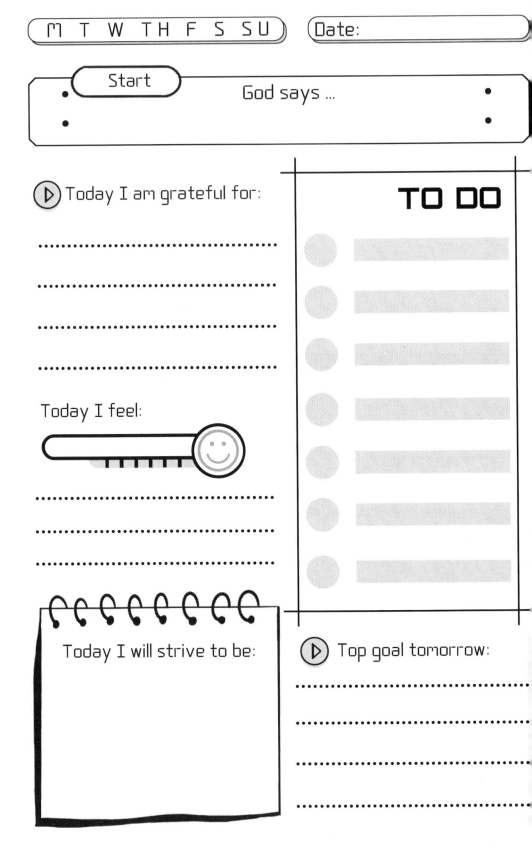   ⬤ ▬▬▬▬▬▬▬▬▬

....   ⬤ ▬▬▬▬▬▬▬▬▬

....

....

Today I will strive to be: ▷ Top goal tomorrow:

                                      ....

                                      ....

                                      ....

                                      ....

M T W TH F S SU)   (Date:

Start
God says ...

▷ Today I am grateful for:

....

....

....

....

Today I feel:

....

....

....

TO DO

Today I will strive to be:

▷ Top goal tomorrow:

....

....

....

....

M T W TH F S SU   Date:

Start   God says ...

-
-

-
-

▷ Today I am grateful for:

....

....

....

....

Today I feel:

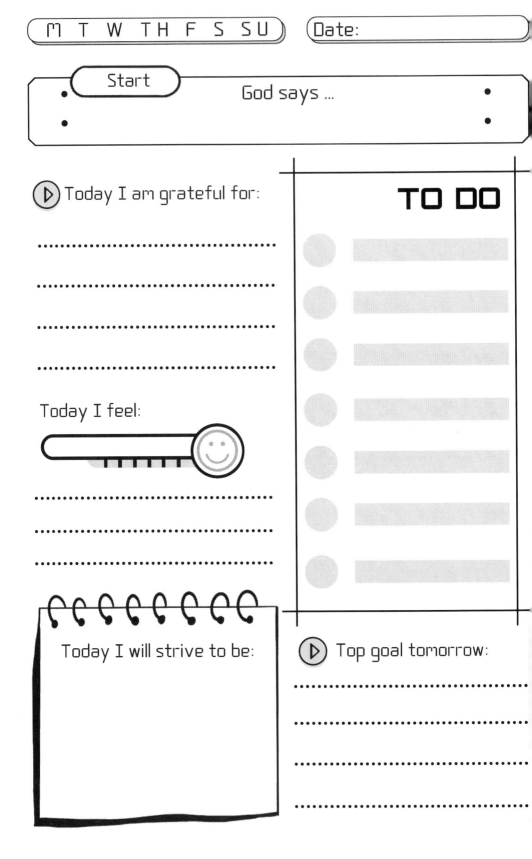

....

....

....

Today I will strive to be:

TO DO

▷ Top goal tomorrow:

....

....

....

....

M T W TH F S SU   Date:

Start   God says ...
•
•   •
                                               •

▷ Today I am grateful for: **TO DO**

....

....

....

....

Today I feel:

....

....

....

Today I will strive to be: ▷ Top goal tomorrow:

....

....

....

....

M T W TH F S SU Date:

Start
God says ...

▷ Today I am grateful for:

....

....

....

....

Today I feel:

:)

....

....

....

TO DO

Today I will strive to be:

▷ Top goal tomorrow:

....

....

....

....

M T W TH F S SU

Date:

Start

God says ...

▷ Today I am grateful for:

....

....

....

....

Today I feel:

....

....

....

TO DO

Today I will strive to be:

▷ Top goal tomorrow:

....

....

....

....

M T W TH F S SU) (Date:

Start
God says ...

(▷) Today I am grateful for:

....

....

....

....

Today I feel:

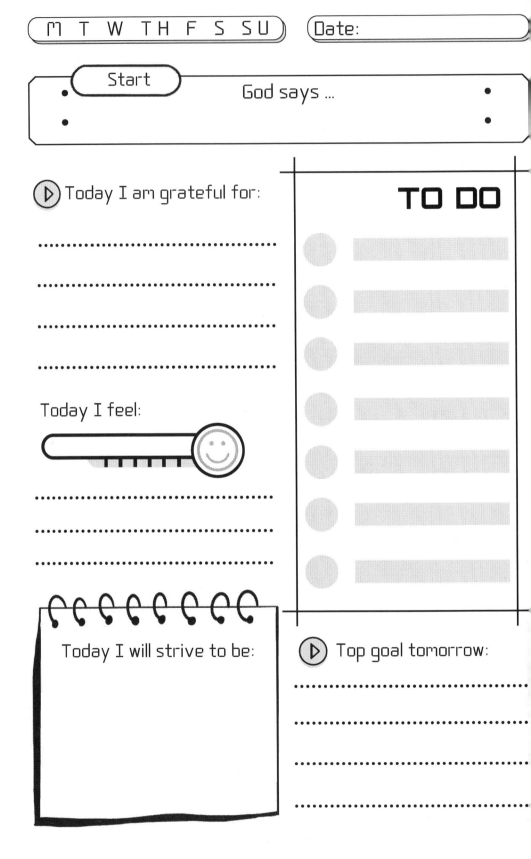

....

....

....

TO DO

Today I will strive to be:

(▷) Top goal tomorrow:

....

....

....

....

M T W TH F S SU   Date:

Start

God says ...

(▷) Today I am grateful for:

....

....

....

....

Today I feel:

....

....

....

TO DO

Today I will strive to be:

(▷) Top goal tomorrow:

....

....

....

....

(M T W TH F S SU) (Date:)

Start

God says ...

- •
- •
- •

- •
- •

▷ Today I am grateful for:

....

....

....

....

Today I feel:

Today I will strive to be:

TO DO

▷ Top goal tomorrow:

....

....

....

....

M T W TH F S SU   Date:

God says ...

▷ Today I am grateful for:

....

....

....

....

Today I feel:

....

....

....

TO DO

Today I will strive to be:

▷ Top goal tomorrow:

....

....

....

....

M T W TH F S SU   Date:

Start   God says ...

▷ Today I am grateful for:

....

....

....

....

Today I feel:

....

....

....

TO DO

Today I will strive to be:

▷ Top goal tomorrow:

....

....

....

....

M T W TH F S SU) (Date:

Start

God says ...

▷ Today I am grateful for:

....

....

....

....

Today I feel:

....

....

....

TO DO

Today I will strive to be:

▷ Top goal tomorrow:

....

....

....

....

M T W TH F S SU   Date:

Start   God says ...

▷ Today I am grateful for:

....

....

....

....

Today I feel:

:)

....

....

....

TO DO

Today I will strive to be:

▷ Top goal tomorrow:

....

....

....

....

M T W TH F S SU   Date:

Start

God says ...

▷ Today I am grateful for:

....

....

....

....

Today I feel:

....

....

....

TO DO

Today I will strive to be:

▷ Top goal tomorrow:

....

....

....

....

M T W TH F S SU   Date:

Start

God says ...

▷ Today I am grateful for:

....

....

....

....

Today I feel:

....

....

....

TO DO

Today I will strive to be:

▷ Top goal tomorrow:

....

....

....

....

M T W TH F S SU) (Date:

Start

God says ...

(▷) Today I am grateful for:

....

....

....

....

Today I feel:

....

....

....

TO DO

Today I will strive to be:

(▷) Top goal tomorrow:

....

....

....

....

M T W TH F S SU   Date:

Start

God says ...

▷ Today I am grateful for:

....

....

....

....

Today I feel:

....

....

....

Today I will strive to be:

TO DO

▷ Top goal tomorrow:

....

....

....

....

M T W TH F S SU   Date:

Start   God says ...

▷ Today I am grateful for:

TO DO

....

....

....

....

Today I feel:

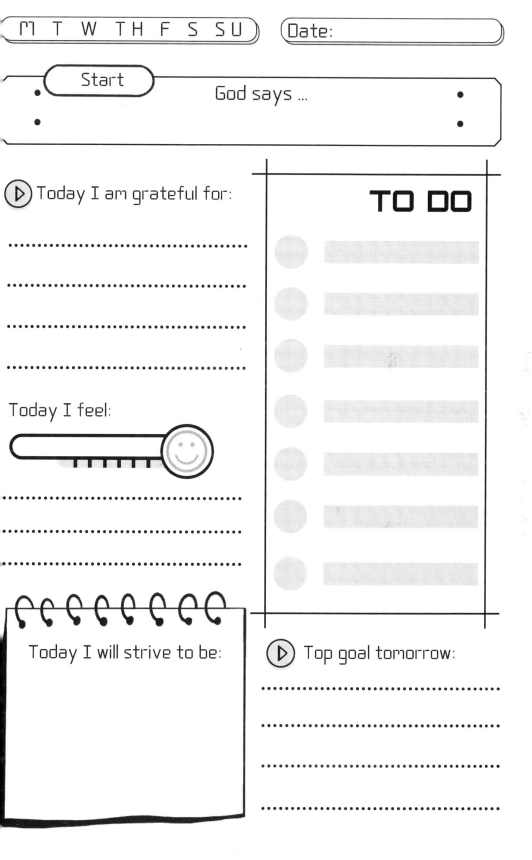

....

....

....

Today I will strive to be: ▷ Top goal tomorrow:

....

....

....

....

M T W TH F S SU)   (Date:

Start

God says ...

▷ Today I am grateful for:

TO DO

....

....

....

....

Today I feel:

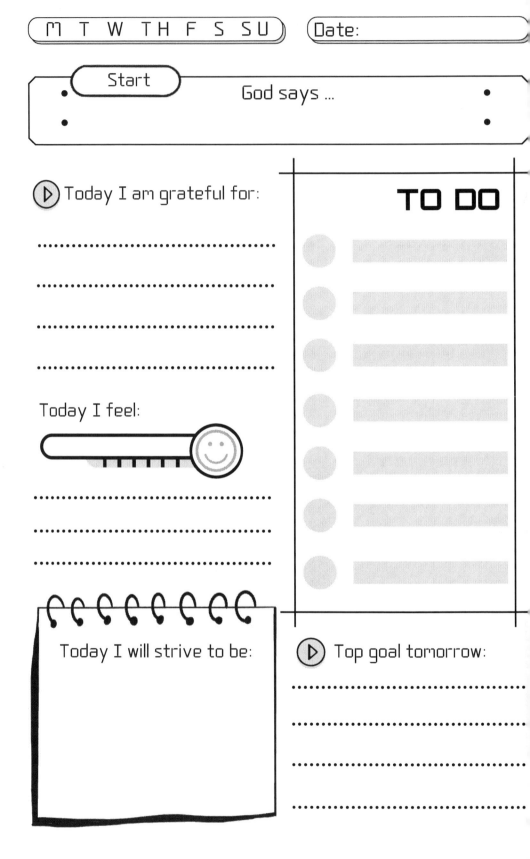

....

....

....

Today I will strive to be:

▷ Top goal tomorrow:

....

....

....

....

M T W TH F S SU) (Date:

Start
-
-

God says ...
-
-

(▷) Today I am grateful for:

....

....

....

....

Today I feel:

....

....

....

TO DO

Today I will strive to be:

(▷) Top goal tomorrow:

....

....

....

....

M T W TH F S SU

Date:

Start

God says ...

▷ Today I am grateful for:

....

....

....

....

Today I feel:

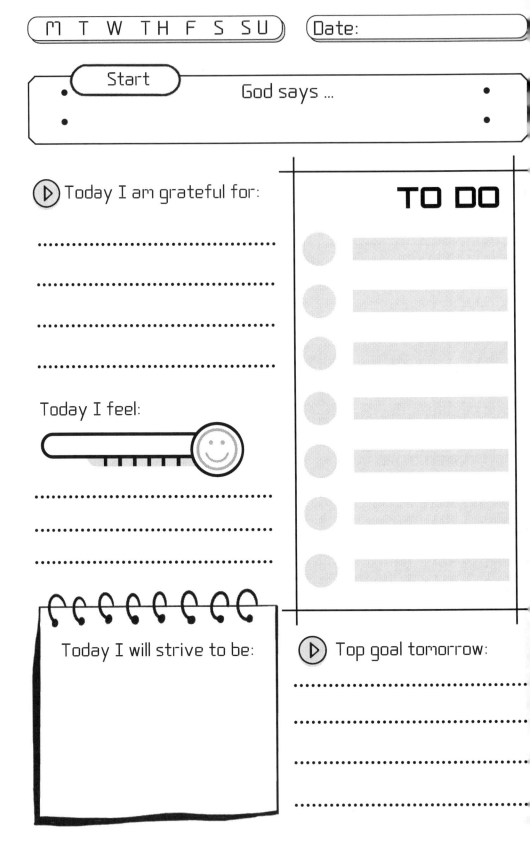

....

....

....

TO DO

Today I will strive to be:

▷ Top goal tomorrow:

....

....

....

....

M T W TH F S SU   Date:

Start
God says ...
•   •
•   •

▷ Today I am grateful for:

....
....
....
....

Today I feel:

....
....
....

TO DO

Today I will strive to be:

▷ Top goal tomorrow:

....
....
....
....

(M T W TH F S SU) (Date: _____)

Start

God says ...
•
•
•
                                    •
                                    •

▷ Today I am grateful for:

....
....
....
....

Today I feel:

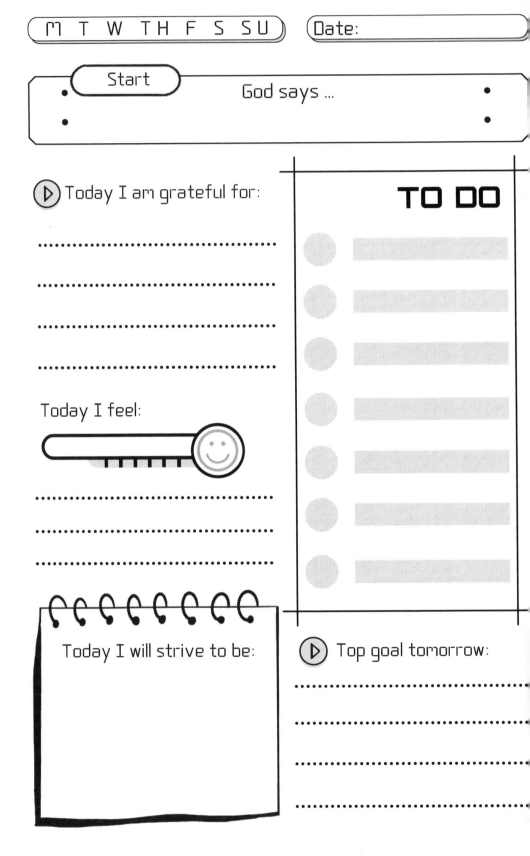

....
....
....

Today I will strive to be:

TO DO

Top goal tomorrow:

....
....
....
....

M T W TH F S SU   Date:

Start   God says ...

▷ Today I am grateful for: TO DO

....

....

....

....

Today I feel:

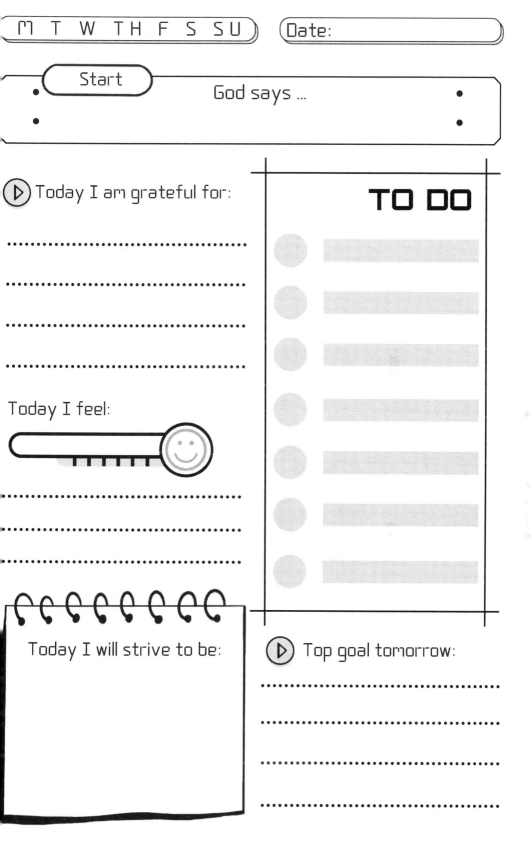

....

....

....

Today I will strive to be: ▷ Top goal tomorrow:

....

....

....

....

M T W TH F S SU   Date:

Start   God says ...

▷ Today I am grateful for:

....

....

....

....

Today I feel:

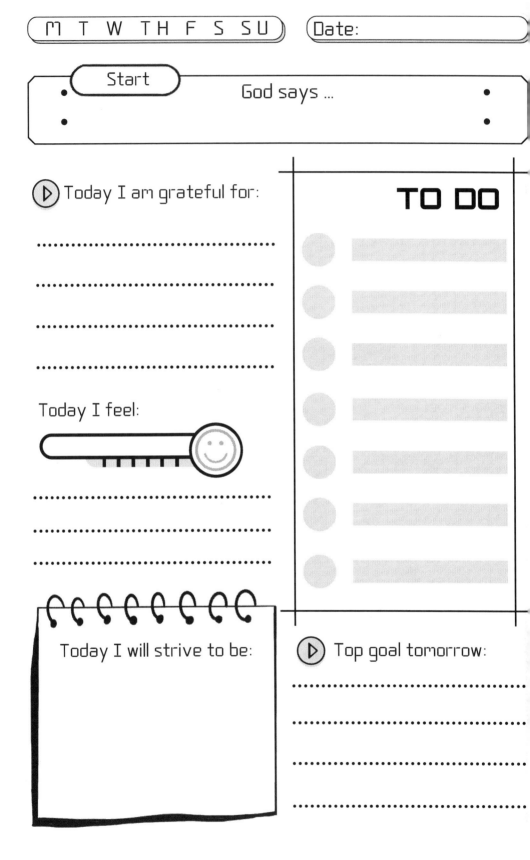

....

....

....

TO DO

Today I will strive to be:

▷ Top goal tomorrow:

....

....

....

....

M T W TH F S SU   Date:

Start   God says ...
-
-

▷ Today I am grateful for:

....

....

....

....

Today I feel:

:)

....

....

....

TO DO

-
-
-
-
-
-
-

Today I will strive to be:

▷ Top goal tomorrow:

....

....

....

....

M T W TH F S SU

Date:

Start

God says ...

-
-
-

▷ Today I am grateful for:

....
....
....
....

Today I feel:

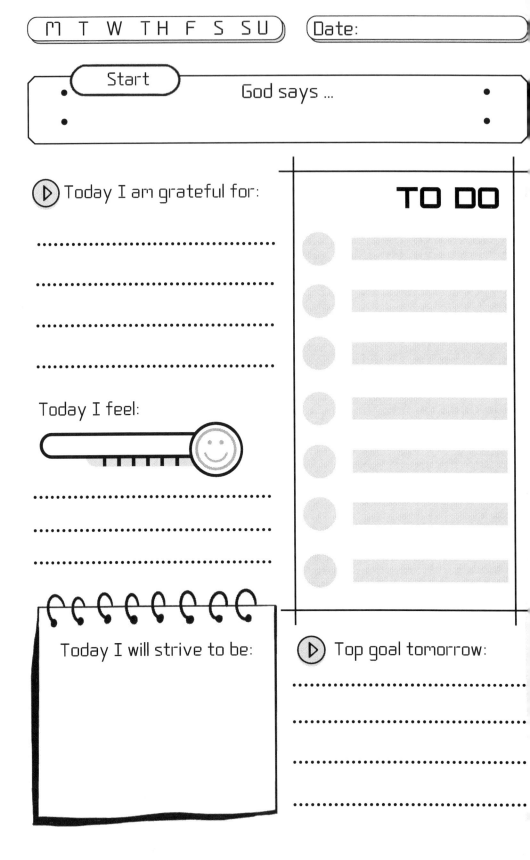

....
....
....

TO DO

Today I will strive to be:

▷ Top goal tomorrow:

....
....
....
....

M T W TH F S SU   Date:

Start

God says ...

▷ Today I am grateful for:

....

....

....

....

Today I feel:

:-)

....

....

....

TO DO

Today I will strive to be:

▷ Top goal tomorrow:

....

....

....

....

M T W TH F S SU   Date:

▷ Today I am grateful for:

....
....
....
....

Today I feel:

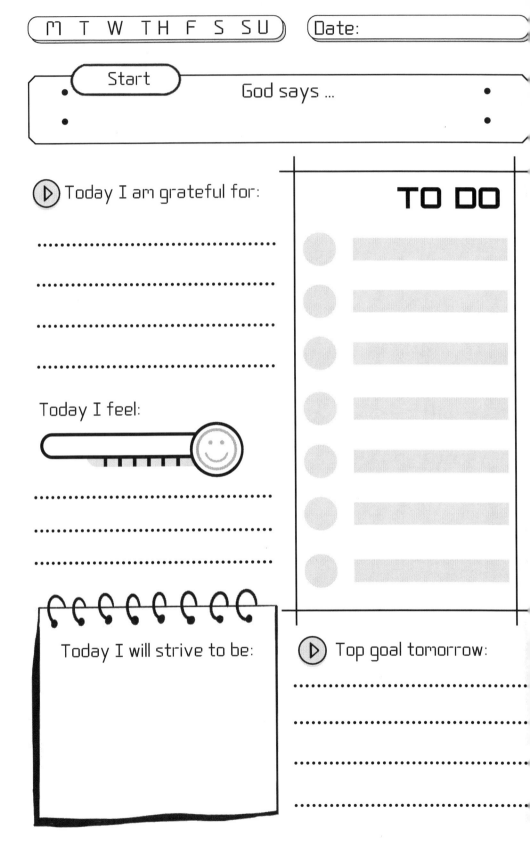

....
....
....

TO DO

Today I will strive to be:

▷ Top goal tomorrow:

....
....
....
....

M T W TH F S SU   Date:

Start

▷ Today I am grateful for:

....

....

....

....

Today I feel:

....

....

....

TO DO

Today I will strive to be:

▷ Top goal tomorrow:

....

....

....

....

Start

God says ...

▷ Today I am grateful for:

....

....

....

....

Today I feel:

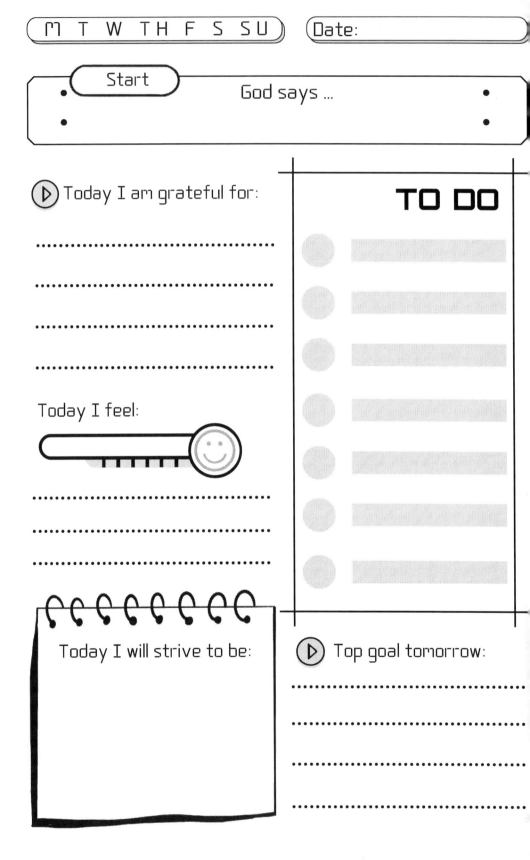

....

....

....

TO DO

Today I will strive to be:

▷ Top goal tomorrow:

....

....

....

....

M T W TH F S SU

Date:

Start

God says ...

▶ Today I am grateful for:

....

....

....

....

Today I feel:

....

....

....

TO DO

Today I will strive to be:

▶ Top goal tomorrow:

....

....

....

....

M T W TH F S SU   Date:

God says ...

▷ Today I am grateful for:

....

....

....

....

Today I feel:

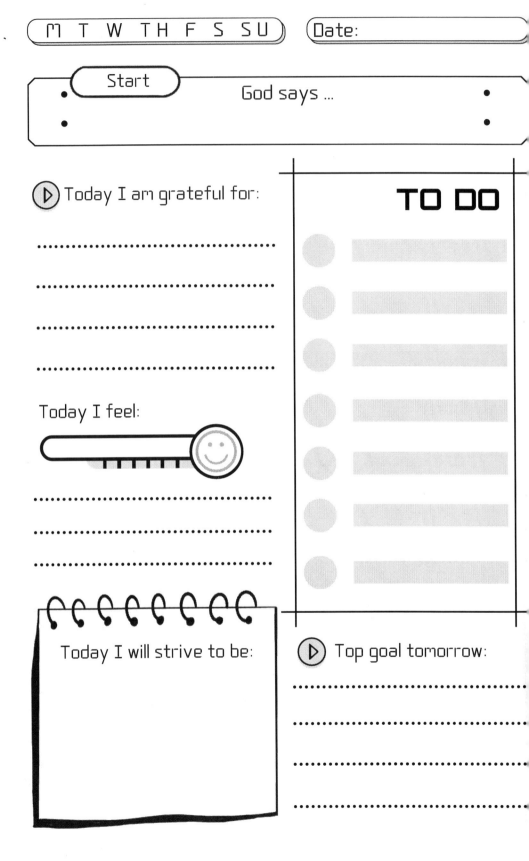

....

....

....

TO DO

Today I will strive to be:

▷ Top goal tomorrow:

....

....

....

....

M T W TH F S SU

Date:

Start

God says ...
-
-
-
-

 Today I am grateful for:

....

....

....

....

Today I feel:

....

....

....

Today I will strive to be:

TO DO

 Top goal tomorrow:

....

....

....

....

M T W TH F S SU   Date:

Start   God says ...
•   •
•   •

▷ Today I am grateful for: **TO DO**

....   ○ ▭
....   ○ ▭
....   ○ ▭
....   ○ ▭

Today I feel: ○ ▭

....   ○ ▭
....   ○ ▭
....

Today I will strive to be: ▷ Top goal tomorrow:

....
....
....
....

M T W TH F S SU   Date:

Start
-
-

God says ...
-
-

▷ Today I am grateful for:

....

....

....

....

Today I feel:

....

....

....

TO DO

Today I will strive to be:

▷ Top goal tomorrow:

....

....

....

....

M T W TH F S SU

Date:

Start

God says ...

▷ Today I am grateful for:

....

....

....

....

Today I feel:

....

....

....

Today I will strive to be:

TO DO

▷ Top goal tomorrow:

....

....

....

....

M T W TH F S SU   Date:

Start

God says ...

▷ Today I am grateful for:

TO DO

....

....

....

....

Today I feel:

....

....

....

Today I will strive to be:

▷ Top goal tomorrow:

....

....

....

....

M T W TH F S SU   Date:

Start   God says ...

▷ Today I am grateful for:

....

....

....

....

Today I feel:

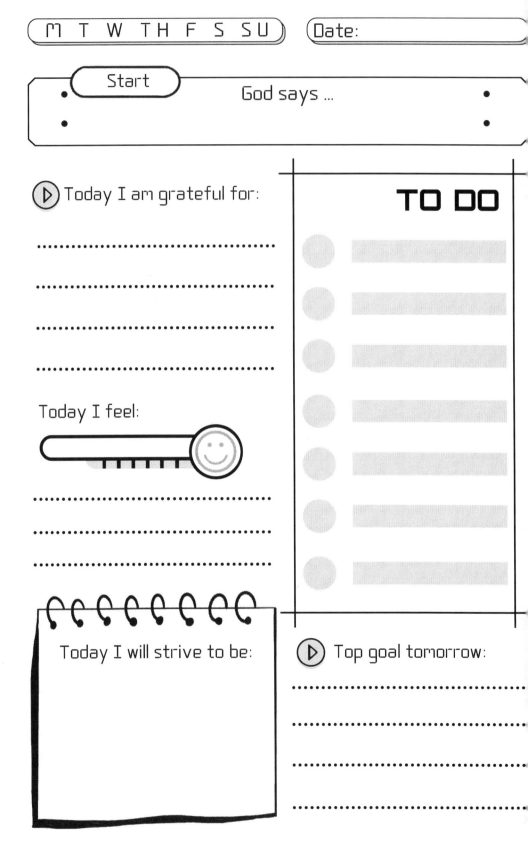

....

....

....

TO DO

Today I will strive to be:

▷ Top goal tomorrow:

....

....

....

....

M T W TH F S SU   Date:

Start   God says ...

▷ Today I am grateful for: **TO DO**

....

....

....

....

Today I feel:

....

....

....

Today I will strive to be: ▷ Top goal tomorrow:

....

....

....

....

M T W TH F S SU   Date:

Start

God says ...

▷ Today I am grateful for:

....

....

....

....

Today I feel:

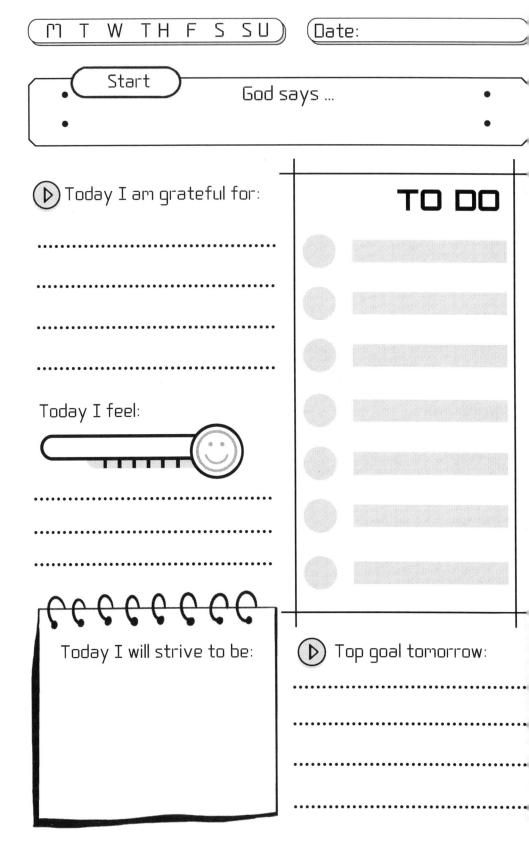

....

....

....

TO DO

Today I will strive to be:

▷ Top goal tomorrow:

....

....

....

....

M T W TH F S SU   Date:

Start

God says ...

-
-

-
-

▷ Today I am grateful for:

....

....

....

....

Today I feel:

....

....

....

TO DO

Today I will strive to be:

▷ Top goal tomorrow:

....

....

....

....

M T W TH F S SU

Date:

Start

God says ...

-
-
-

▷ Today I am grateful for:

....

....

....

....

TO DO

Today I feel:

....

....

....

Today I will strive to be:

▷ Top goal tomorrow:

....

....

....

....

M T W TH F S SU   Date:

Start

God says ...
-
-
  -
  -

▷ Today I am grateful for:

....
....
....
....

Today I feel:

....
....
....

Today I will strive to be:

TO DO

▷ Top goal tomorrow:

....
....
....
....

M T W TH F S SU   Date:

Start

God says ...

▷ Today I am grateful for:

TO DO

....

....

....

....

Today I feel:

😊

....

....

....

Today I will strive to be:

▷ Top goal tomorrow:

....

....

....

....

M T W TH F S SU   Date:

Start
God says ...

Today I am grateful for:

....

....

....

....

Today I feel:

....

....

....

TO DO

Today I will strive to be:

Top goal tomorrow:

....

....

....

....

M T W TH F S SU) (Date:

Start
God says ...

▷ Today I am grateful for:

....

....

....

....

Today I feel:

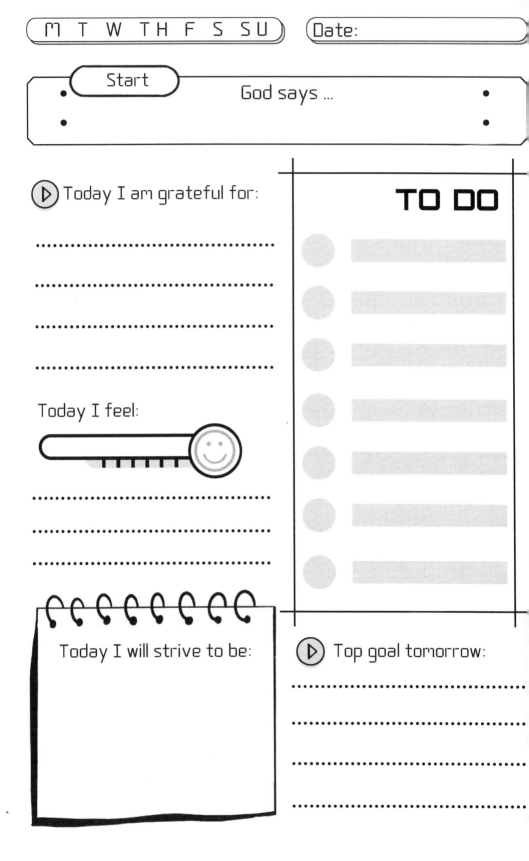

....

....

....

TO DO

Today I will strive to be:

▷ Top goal tomorrow:

....

....

....

....

M T W TH F S SU   Date:

Start

God says ...

-
-
-
-

▷ Today I am grateful for:

....

....

....

....

Today I feel:

....

....

....

TO DO

Today I will strive to be:

▷ Top goal tomorrow:

....

....

....

....

M T W TH F S SU   Date:

Start

God says ...

▷ Today I am grateful for:

....
....
....
....

Today I feel:

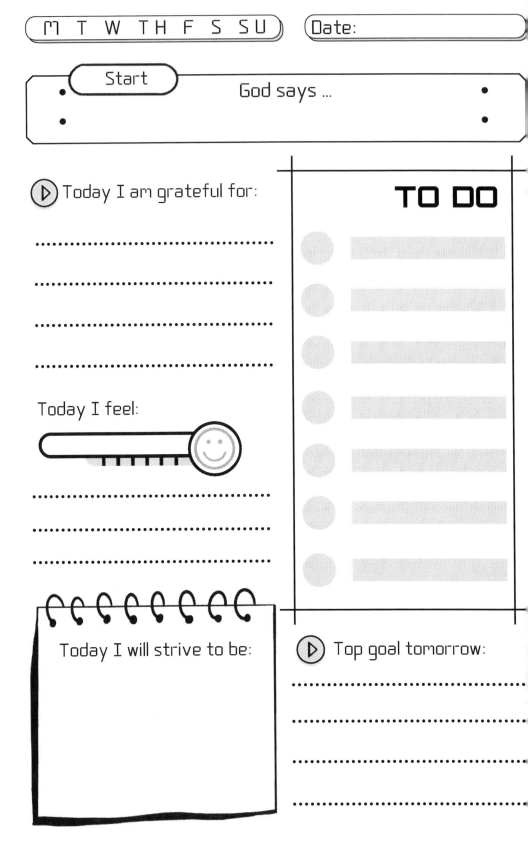

....
....
....

TO DO

Today I will strive to be:

▷ Top goal tomorrow:

....
....
....
....

M T W TH F S SU   Date:

Start
•
•   God says ...   •
                                                            •

▷ Today I am grateful for: **TO DO**

....   ○ ▬▬▬▬▬▬▬▬

....   ○ ▬▬▬▬▬▬▬▬

....   ○ ▬▬▬▬▬▬▬▬

....   ○ ▬▬▬▬▬▬▬▬

Today I feel: ○ ▬▬▬▬▬▬▬▬

☺   ○ ▬▬▬▬▬▬▬▬

....   ○ ▬▬▬▬▬▬▬▬

....

....

Today I will strive to be: ▷ Top goal tomorrow:

                                         ....

                                         ....

                                         ....

                                         ....

M T W TH F S SU   Date:

Start

God says ...

▷ Today I am grateful for:

....

....

....

....

Today I feel:

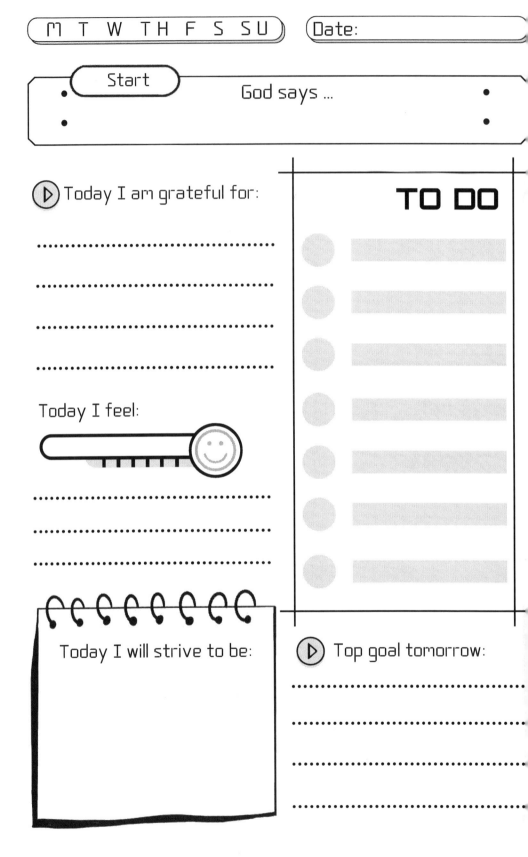

....

....

....

TO DO

Today I will strive to be:

▷ Top goal tomorrow:

....

....

....

....

M T W TH F S SU   Date:

Start

God says ...

▷ Today I am grateful for:

....

....

....

....

Today I feel:

....

....

....

TO DO

Today I will strive to be:

▷ Top goal tomorrow:

....

....

....

....

M T W TH F S SU   Date:

Start   God says ...
-
-
-

▷ Today I am grateful for:

....

....

....

....

Today I feel:

....

....

....

TO DO

Today I will strive to be:

▷ Top goal tomorrow:

....

....

....

....

M T W TH F S SU) (Date:

Start

God says ...

·
·

▷ Today I am grateful for:

....

....

....

....

Today I feel:

....

....

....

Today I will strive to be:

TO DO

▷ Top goal tomorrow:

....

....

....

....

M T W TH F S SU   Date:

Start   God says ...

▷ Today I am grateful for:

....

....

....

....

Today I feel:

....

....

....

Today I will strive to be:

TO DO

▷ Top goal tomorrow:

....

....

....

....

M T W TH F S SU) (Date:

Start

God says ...

-
-
-
-

▷ Today I am grateful for:

....
....
....
....

Today I feel:

....
....
....

Today I will strive to be:

TO DO

▷ Top goal tomorrow:

....
....
....
....

M T W TH F S SU | Date:

Start | God says ...
-
-
-
-

▷ Today I am grateful for:

....

....

....

....

Today I feel:

....

....

....

Today I will strive to be:

TO DO

-
-
-
-
-
-
-

▷ Top goal tomorrow:

....

....

....

....

M T W TH F S SU) (Date:

Start) ──────── God says ...
• •
• •

▷ Today I am grateful for:

....

....

....

....

Today I feel:

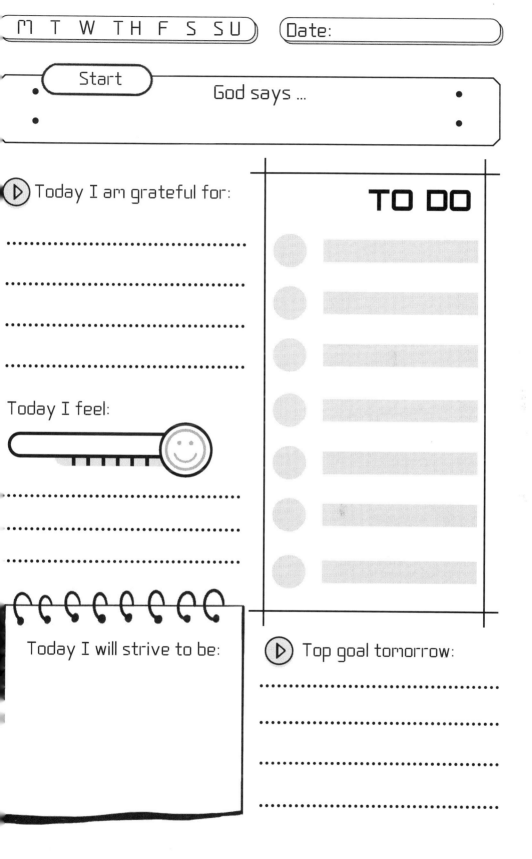

....

....

....

TO DO

Today I will strive to be:

▷ Top goal tomorrow:

....

....

....

....

M T W TH F S SU

Date:

Start

God says ...

▷ Today I am grateful for:

....

....

....

....

Today I feel:

....

....

....

TO DO

Today I will strive to be:

▷ Top goal tomorrow:

....

....

....

....

M T W TH F S SU   Date:

Start

God says ...

▷ Today I am grateful for:

TO DO

....

....

....

....

Today I feel:

....

....

....

Today I will strive to be:

▷ Top goal tomorrow:

....

....

....

....

M T W TH F S SU   Date:

Start

God says ...
-
-
-
-

▷ Today I am grateful for:

....

....

....

....

Today I feel:

....

....

....

Today I will strive to be:

TO DO

▷ Top goal tomorrow:

....

....

....

....

M T W TH F S SU   Date:

Start
God says ...
•   •
•   •

▷ Today I am grateful for:

....

....

....

....

Today I feel:

😊

....

....

....

Today I will strive to be:

TO DO

▷ Top goal tomorrow:

....

....

....

....

M T W TH F S SU   Date:

Start   God says ...
•   •
•   •

▷ Today I am grateful for:

....

....

....

....

Today I feel:

🙂

....

....

....

Today I will strive to be:

TO DO

▷ Top goal tomorrow:

....

....

....

....

M T W TH F S SU   Date:

Start

•
•

God says ...

•
•

▷ Today I am grateful for:

....

....

....

....

Today I feel:

....

....

....

TO DO

Today I will strive to be:

▷ Top goal tomorrow:

....

....

....

....

M T W TH F S SU   Date:

Start

God says ...

▷ Today I am grateful for:

....

....

....

....

Today I feel:

😊

....

....

....

TO DO

Today I will strive to be:

▷ Top goal tomorrow:

....

....

....

....

M T W TH F S SU   Date:

Start

God says ...

▷ Today I am grateful for:

....

....

....

....

Today I feel:

....

....

....

TO DO

Today I will strive to be:

▷ Top goal tomorrow:

....

....

....

....

M T W TH F S SU   Date:

Start

God says ...
-
-
-
-

▶ Today I am grateful for:

....

....

....

....

Today I feel:

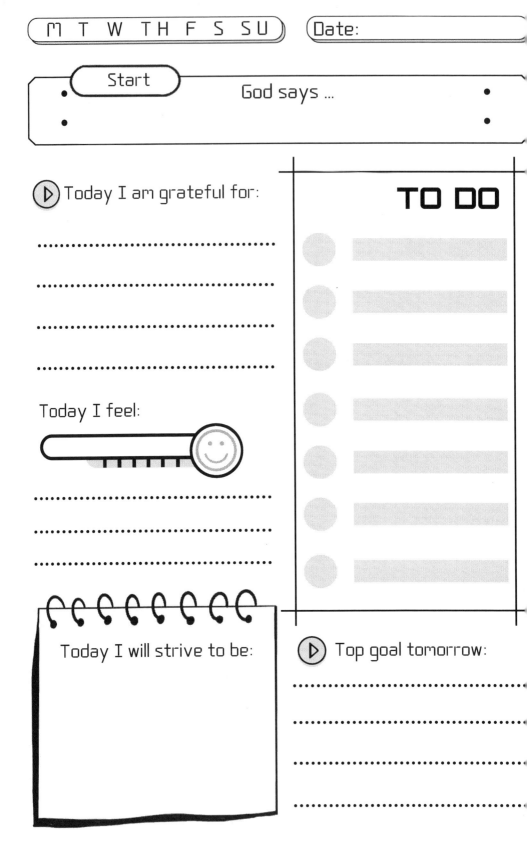

....

....

....

TO DO

Today I will strive to be:

▶ Top goal tomorrow:

....

....

....

....

M T W TH F S SU

Date:

God says ...

-
-

▷ Today I am grateful for:

....

....

....

....

Today I feel:

....

....

....

Today I will strive to be:

TO DO

○ ▭▭▭▭▭▭▭▭

○ ▭▭▭▭▭▭▭▭

○ ▭▭▭▭▭▭▭▭

○ ▭▭▭▭▭▭▭▭

○ ▭▭▭▭▭▭▭▭

○ ▭▭▭▭▭▭▭▭

○ ▭▭▭▭▭▭▭▭

▷ Top goal tomorrow:

....

....

....

....

M T W TH F S SU   Date:

Start

God says ...

▶ Today I am grateful for:

....

....

....

....

Today I feel:

....

....

....

TO DO

Today I will strive to be:

▶ Top goal tomorrow:

....

....

....

....

M T W TH F S SU   Date:

Start

God says ...

-
-

-
-

▷ Today I am grateful for:

....

....

....

....

Today I feel:

....

....

....

TO DO

Today I will strive to be:

▷ Top goal tomorrow:

....

....

....

....

M T W TH F S SU

Date:

Start

God says ...

▷ Today I am grateful for:

....

....

....

....

Today I feel:

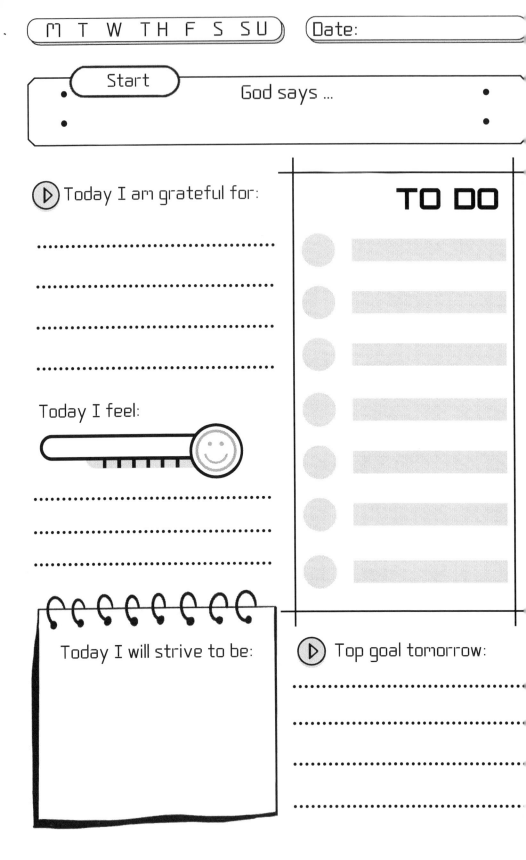

....

....

....

TO DO

Today I will strive to be:

▷ Top goal tomorrow:

....

....

....

....

M T W TH F S SU   Date:

Start
God says ...
•
•   •
                                               •

▷ Today I am grateful for:

....

....

....

....

Today I feel:

....

....

....

TO DO

Today I will strive to be:

▷ Top goal tomorrow:

....

....

....

....

M T W TH F S SU   Date:

Start   God says ...
•   •
•   •

▷ Today I am grateful for:

....

....

....

....

TO DO

Today I feel:

☺

....

....

....

Today I will strive to be:

▷ Top goal tomorrow:

....

....

....

....

M T W TH F S SU   Date:

Start

God says ...

▷ Today I am grateful for:

....

....

....

....

Today I feel:

☺

....

....

....

Today I will strive to be:

TO DO

▷ Top goal tomorrow:

....

....

....

....

M T W TH F S SU | Date:

Start

God says ...

-
-

▷ Today I am grateful for:

....

....

....

....

Today I feel:

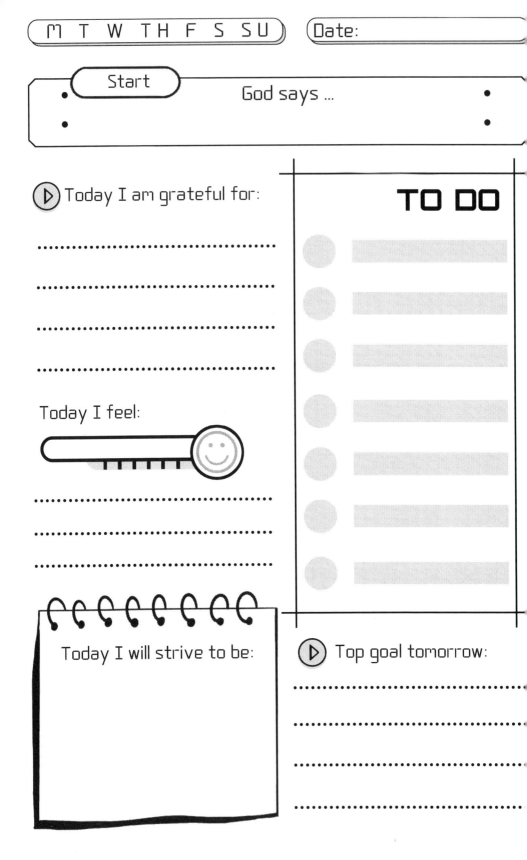

....

....

....

Today I will strive to be:

TO DO

-
-
-
-
-
-
-

▷ Top goal tomorrow:

....

....

....

....

M T W TH F S SU   Date:

Start   God says ...
•   •
•   •

▷ Today I am grateful for:

....

....

....

....

Today I feel:

....

....

....

TO DO

Today I will strive to be:

▷ Top goal tomorrow:

....

....

....

....

M T W TH F S SU

Date:

Start

God says ...

▷ Today I am grateful for:

....

....

....

....

Today I feel:

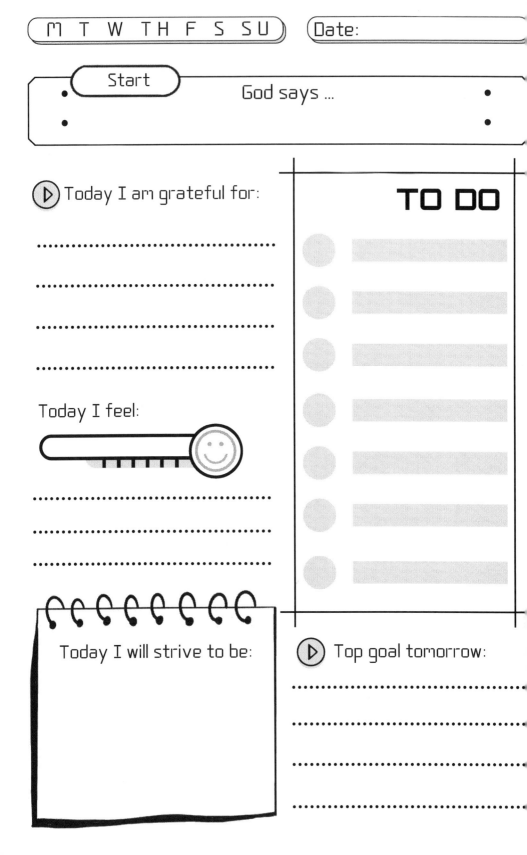

....

....

....

Today I will strive to be:

TO DO

▷ Top goal tomorrow:

....

....

....

....

M T W TH F S SU   Date:

Start

God says ...

▷ Today I am grateful for:

....

....

....

....

Today I feel:

☺

....

....

....

Today I will strive to be:

TO DO

▷ Top goal tomorrow:

....

....

....

....

M T W TH F S SU   Date:

God says ...

-
-

▷ Today I am grateful for:

....
....
....
....

Today I feel:

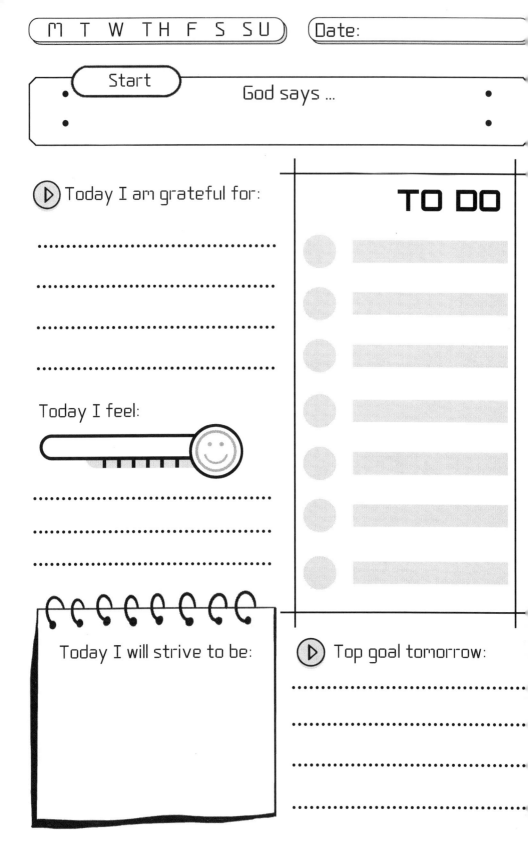

....
....
....

Today I will strive to be:

TO DO

▷ Top goal tomorrow:

....
....
....
....

M T W TH F S SU   Date:

Start
God says ...

▷ Today I am grateful for:

....

....

....

....

Today I feel:

....

....

....

TO DO

Today I will strive to be:

▷ Top goal tomorrow:

....

....

....

....

M T W TH F S SU   Date:

Start

God says ...

▷ Today I am grateful for:

....

....

....

....

Today I feel:

....

....

....

TO DO

Today I will strive to be:

▷ Top goal tomorrow:

....

....

....

....

Made in the USA
Columbia, SC
07 December 2024

48666848R00067